THE ENCAUSTIC ART
PROJECT BOOK

SEARCH PRESS

Art is about being. This book is dedicated to all those who find the courage to explore, discover and refresh their vision — again, and again, and again.

THE ENCAUSTIC ART PROJECT BOOK

Michael Bossom

SEARCH PRESS

This Edition published in Great Britain in 2016 by
Search Press Limited
Wellwood, North Farm Road,
Tunbridge Wells, Kent TN2 3DR

Originally published in Great Britain 2002
Reprinted 2005, 2007, 2008, 2010, 2011, 2012

ISBN: 978-1-78221-421-2

Suppliers
For details of suppliers, please visit the
Search Press website: www.searchpress.com

Publisher's note
All the step-by-step photographs in this book feature the
author, Michael Bossom, demonstrating encaustic art.
No models have been used.

Printed in Malaysia

Special thanks to Roz, Ally and
Lotti, without whom this book
would not exist. Also to Shona,
whose support and love makes
all things possible. Finally to
you, the reader, who makes
the effort worthwhile and who
stimulates my creativity.

Cover: **New Song**
*The author's own mix of wax colour,
applied to a rigid surface with the iron
and embellished with a stylus drawing
tip.*

Page 1: **Alzuree**
Abstract on crumpled paper.

Pages 2-3: **Floral Chorus**
*Encaustic printed on silk and over-
painted using silk colour, with salt
effects — see pages 84-85.*

Page 5: **Stained glass design**
*Geometric design in luminous wax
colours outlined with black — see
pages 46-47.*

CONTENTS

6   Introduction

10   Materials and equipment
wax • surfaces

16   Using colour

20   Basic techniques
dabbing • shuffling
wriggling • rattling

24   Composition
monochromatic balance

28   Landscapes
adding details • trees
simple landscape

40   Abstract designs
marquetry • patchwork mosaic
stained glass

48   Silhouetting

50   Hot air work

54   Different surfaces
semi-absorbent • crushed paper
textured board • coloured card
parchment paper • watercolour paper
tissue paper • composite board

82   Printing and over-painting
silk over-painting • fabric collage
embroidered design

90   Wax stamping

93   Borders and frames

96   Index

INTRODUCTION

Encaustic art is an unusual and different way to create beautiful works of art; an exciting and versatile medium which allows people of all abilities to release their creative potential.

The technique involves coloured waxes which are melted, applied to various surfaces and allowed to cool. The reason encaustic art is such a different way to create works of art is that the waxes can be re-melted as often as you like. You can change your artwork at any time – almost like magic – with just a touch of your iron. This facility for change is especially valuable for beginners, who may lack confidence in their artistic ability. Being able to 'un-freeze' what you have done enables bold exploration and inspires a wonderful sense of creative confidence. Try it, and you will know exactly what I mean.

While encaustic art is ideal for those who are just beginning to explore their creativity, it can also be useful for practised artists. Many have found that it is the perfect medium for creative exploration, experimentation and doodles. These free, rapidly-produced pieces can be the inspiration for more carefully formed artwork.

The word encaustic, which means *to burn in*, relates to the use of heat as the solvent for coloured waxes – a technique developed many thousands of years ago. Ancient peoples made 'soul portraits' from wax and earth pigments, which were applied to thin wooden panels and bound to the mummified bodies of those whose families could afford this privileged service. The heat source was originally charcoal, but thermostatically-controlled modern electric tools have prompted a renewal of interest in encaustic art.

In painting, most media are worked wet on a supporting surface, given time to dry, and are then considered finished, with limited potential for alteration. This is not the case with encaustic wax, which behaves as a liquid when heated but as a solid when cool. This unusual quality, combined with the brilliance of the colours, inspires a fresh fascination every time it is used. The intermingling colours flow under the heated iron to emerge in intriguing and unplanned ways. Basic effects can be controlled with practice, but the intrinsic forms and colour blends are unique every time.

You may start with abstracts which are no more than a pleasing mess, or perhaps enjoy finding forms in the colours and shapes so easily produced by working with the iron. This fun, accessible approach is absorbing and surprising in equal measure. It can be a great release for the imagination, and is extremely therapeutic. As an encaustic art beginner, you do not need to know what to *do*, you just need to start *doing* and enjoy what happens. Time spent working with encaustic art can seem to pass all too quickly. Many people have switched on an iron, melted some wax and realised – hours later – that they have somehow entered this mysterious timeless zone.

Some of the details you may wish to include in your finished artwork – such as flowers and trees – will require an element of study, to find a way to represent

Abstract on absorbent paper

*Bright, bold colours and interesting forms are easy to achieve
applying the molten wax colours with the iron. On non-absorbent
surfaces, the wax can be re-tooled into a new set of forms and
hues. When absorbent paper is used, the colour initially applied
penetrates the surface, so it cannot be removed. As in this case,
dramatic effects can be achieved by using the stylus to embellish
the work, or darker colours can be added with the iron.*

these elements in a way which communicates their essence. At first, this is about simplifying shapes and keeping colours to a minimum. As your creative ability grows, you may wish to develop a more controlled technique, and include more detail in your finished artworks. This is especially likely with more experienced painters, who may prefer to have greater control over the finished result. Painting is often viewed as drawing in colour, with a structured, planned approach to the subject-matter. For this type of approach, using a low-heat stylus tool instead of an iron will allow you to 'draw' your work.

Some dictionaries define craft as 'skill' and art as 'skill with imagination'. But I prefer to regard art as a reflection of being: a reaction to and interaction with all that is experienced in life. If you follow my definition, every human being is already artistic because he or she was born an individual and is unique. Whatever your starting point or direction, the special qualities of encaustic art can stimulate your creativity and act as a catalyst for your imagination.

The following pages offer help, insight and some suggested approaches to this absorbing and rewarding art form. Begin with lots of small-scale experiments and move on to larger pieces as your skills and ambition develop. Often, when you are not completely satisfied with an artwork, you can find areas you do like. Cut these out and use them in another piece, or re-melt and re-work the areas you are not happy with.

So to begin. You need waxes, tools and surfaces, a grasp of basic techniques and approaches, plus ideas. You do not need special skills, though any you develop will serve you well. If you are brave enough to step out into the unknown you will find an adventure waiting for you. This adventure will take you on a journey through the images you produce, and as you are always in control it is your journey. When you switch on the iron, you embark on a creative process that is fresh every time. With encaustic art, creativity can be a never-ending story.

Michael Bossom

Artist's statement

Creative artists gather the tools and materials that inspire them and begin the creative process. The artist is infused with creative potential. Boundaries blur. Hands reach out; eyes search eagerly; the mind is keenly aware, and the heart beats with anticipation. Realisation continues as, assisted by the skills of its creator, the work becomes manifest, its qualities a reflection of the artist's involvement. What skill? What honing? What insight? What inspiration, integrity or intent? The instinctive response of others will be the most truthful.

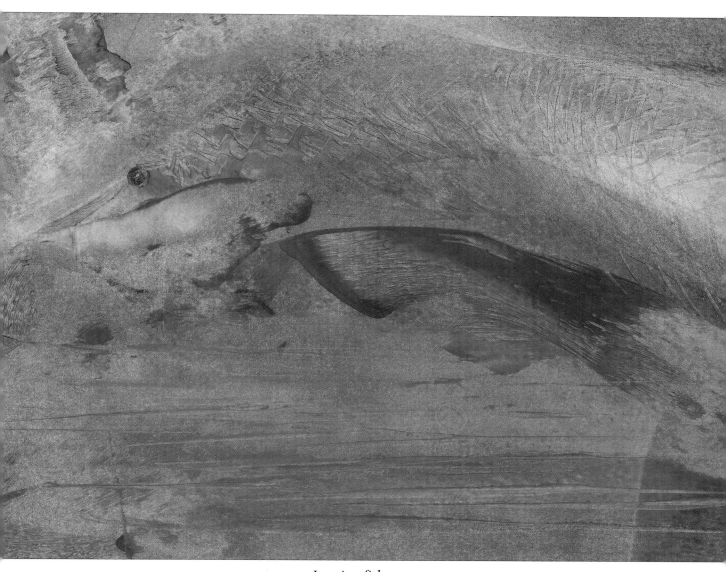

Leaping fish
*Encaustic art can be full of surprises, and this fish seemed
mysteriously to appear as I worked. I simply helped the illusion
by adding an eye. The work is on parchment paper.*

MATERIALS AND EQUIPMENT

Any tool that produces a controllable, low heat which can safely melt wax could be used for encaustic art. The most commonly-used tools are:

IRON

A standard travel iron can be used for encaustic art; larger domestic irons are awkward to use and can become too hot. The specially-developed Encaustic Art painting iron is small, light and easy to use. It operates at between 70-80°C (158-176°F) on a low setting, and can also be used as a small hotplate.

STYLUS AND TIPS

The Encaustic Art stylus maintains the correct low temperature. Soldering irons or pyrography (wood burning) tools are too hot. Tips fit into the stylus stem and include a split tip for drawing, a fine wire brush tip for applying, blending and tooling wax, a micro tip (like a tiny trowel) and a slightly larger mini tip. The aluminium mini and micro tips can also be filed into interesting shapes. Other small metal objects, like a screw head or a piece of copper wire, can be inserted to produce interesting effects.

SCRIBER

A metal rod with one pointed end and one end with a blade which is used to scratch through the wax or scrape away layers of colour. Other 'tools' you can try include knife blades, needles, knitting needles and old dental tools.

HAIRDRYER

This must be robust to produce the temperature and air flow needed to liquefy and blow the wax: salon dryers are usually the most durable. The best offer a choice of temperatures and blowing speeds. Round, or round reducing nozzles generally offer the best control. Heat guns and paint strippers can be used, but are not recommended until you are experienced.

MARKER PEN

These can be used both under and over wax colours. Test before using as some inks will smudge if wax is spread over them, and ink applied to a completed work will merge with the wax if you try to re-work it.

CRAFT KNIFE

Use with a cutting mat to cut materials, trim the edges of artwork, or to cut out shapes.

CUTTING MAT

A 'self-healing' plastic mat is ideal: the blade goes into the mat's surface leaving little sign of damage.

SCISSORS

These are essential for clean, accurate cutting.

ADHESIVE

Use the spray type to mount artwork, and stick adhesives and double-sided tape for making cards.

SOFT TISSUE

Avoid the harder domestic type of paper as it may scratch the surface of your artwork.

COMPUTER PAPER

Useful for protecting your work surface from wax.

RULE

Use this to straighten edges or draw straight lines.

PAINTBRUSHES

These can be used to apply molten wax. Avoid nylon as it may melt in the hot wax. Hog's hair is readily available and is not from an endangered species.

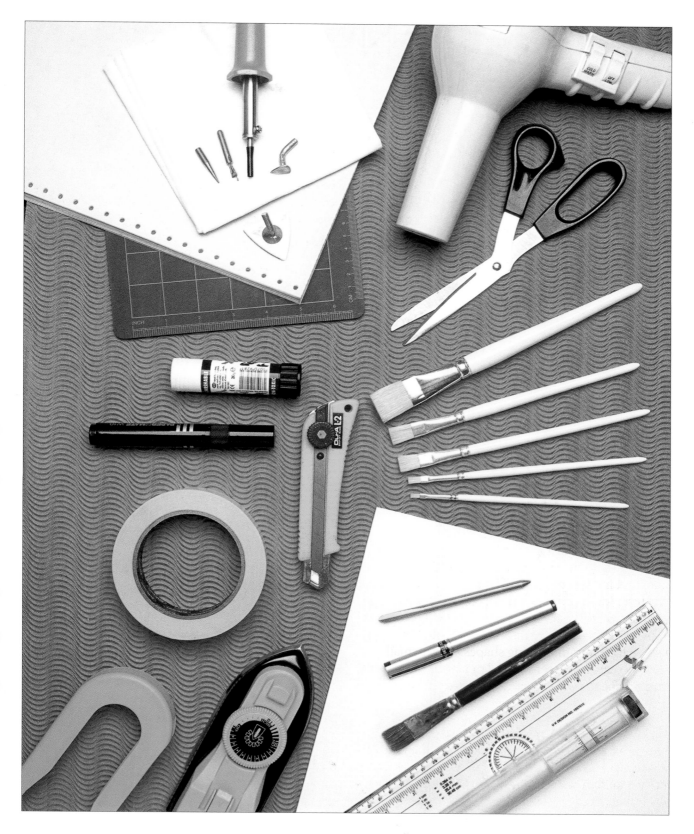

WAX

Wax is a versatile material, which when melted changes from a solid to a liquid. Encaustic art waxes are made from one or more different types of wax, combined with pigments for colour, and sometimes resin. Blending the waxes and/or adding resin raises the melting point, strengthens and improves the adhesion of the resulting medium. This medium is made into wax blocks which are sold ready for use in an enormous range of colours. Reference to 'wax' throughout this book should be taken to mean these ready-to-use encaustic art wax blocks.

Every encaustic paint mixture performs differently, depending on the type and proportions of basic ingredients used. There are too many types of wax to list individually, but a traditional recipe for an encaustic medium – the base mix to which the pigment is added – is 85% beeswax to 15% Damar resin. You will have to test different makes to find which you prefer. It is possible to make your own waxes, but it requires quite a bit of experience. For simplicity, I have used the Stockmar range of waxes for the techniques and artwork in this book.

Stockmar encaustic waxes were developed to high standards of quality, safety and performance. Colours have a melting point of around 65°C (149°F) and a good molten consistency. Pigments used are non-hazardous, and have performed well in tests for light-fastness. When cool, the waxes buff to an attractive sheen. One point to note is that, when a lot of white is included in the mix to form pastel colours, it may affect colour fastness and result in some fading over time.

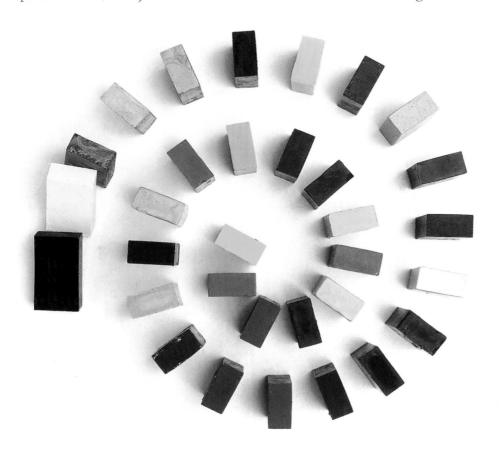

Encaustic waxes
Virtually any colour of wax, in a wide range of consistencies, can be made by mixing wax with different pigments (above). Each pigment has different qualities, and encaustic wax mixes vary greatly. There are many types of commercially-produced wax available, and at first, it is probably wise to stick to one range (see left) which will help to speed up your grasp of the skills needed to achieve work that is controllable and repeatable. It is possible to mix your own wax too.

Clockwise, from top: beeswax, carnauba wax, micro-crystalline wax, paraffin wax, refined beeswax pellets; beeswax pellets.

BEESWAX

A natural product, beeswax varies according to where it was produced. Pollens and oils affect its odour, colour and nature but in general, beeswax melts at about 62°C (144°F). It is the basis of all encaustic paints used in ancient times, and some definitions require its inclusion for a mixture to be a true encaustic medium. Wax blocks produced with beeswax melt at about 65°C (149°F).

PARAFFIN WAX

A cheaper, man-made product derived from oil, this has a cloudy transparent colouring. It has a lower melting point of around 55°C (131°F).

CARNAUBA WAX

Derived from plant leaves, this is a hard, brittle golden or greyish coloured wax with a melting point of around 80°C (176°F). It buffs to a high polish.

MICRO-CRYSTALLINE WAXES

Hard and soft micro-crystalline waxes are used to change the nature of the wax, to make it harder and more brittle or softer and more pliable.

PIGMENTS

These could be described as coloured dirt. Pigments are ground into fine powder and mixed with a medium (wax, oil, gum, etc.) before application. The colour (hue) of the pigment may be very stable and durable over a period of time and is then considered light-fast or permanent. Some pigments are less constant and will fade over time.

DYES

These chemical colours can produce vivid hues, but unfortunately they cannot be considered light-fast.

WAX SEALER

True encaustic wax paint does not really need any form of protection, but for work which is to be handled, e.g. greetings cards, acrylic varnish or sealer may be useful to toughen the surface.

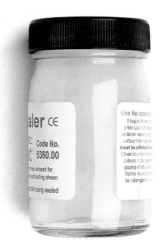

SURFACES

Encaustic waxes can be used on many different surfaces, each offering unique results, as these vary according to the degree of absorption and flexibility of the support material. Lots of experimentation is required to discover whether materials are suitable for your creative applications.

If you use a sealed non-porous paper, the wax will remain on the surface without impregnating the underlying material. This means you will be able to re-work the wax without making the paper dirty, a bit like working on a piece of glass which you can wipe clean. If you use an absorbent material, the wax and colour will penetrate the structure of the material and become lodged in the minute surface voids. This means you will not be able to move the wax around, and the surface will be stained by the colours applied.

The flexibility of your support material has an impact on how you work, and the ways in which you can use your resulting artwork. Thick wax layers may crack if the support surface is too flexible, but rigid support surfaces may also cause problems by restricting the lifting, suction effect produced by the iron.

SUPPORT MATERIALS

Sealed white lightweight card is the best to begin with because it allows easy re-working of the waxes. A white surface reflects all colours of light giving maximum vitality to any translucent colours applied.

The card can be shiny or matt as long as the surface is impermeable to the wax, and as it is flexible it is ideal for iron techniques. Take care not to re-work the card too much; the action of the pigments under the iron can wear down the surface coating, and colours may begin to permeate the underlying material, which will then absorb some colour.

Coloured sealed card can give a very different feeling to an artwork. Black, non-absorbent card is great for pastel colours, which show up in strong contrast against the card. Metallics also look very good on black and provide an even wider range of possibilities. The effect produced by different colours will depend on how the card absorbs or reflects different colours. Translucent green wax will appear black if it is used on red card because red and green are opposite colours in the spectrum; translucent blue wax may appear green if used on a yellow card. Opaque wax colours will not be affected by the colour of the material underneath as light bounces off their surface.

Absorbent cards and **papers** including watercolour paper, parchment paper and mounting board can be used to great effect. You will need to experiment with each type to determine its qualities and the best way to use it. Some surfaces, such as parchment paper, are partly absorbent: colour will enter the fabric of the paper, but only enough to tint it. This can produce interesting effects, and can give a softer finish to the artwork than when a hard, clean, sealed surface is used. A point to remember is that once the papers are saturated with colour, you will not usually be able to wipe them clean or remove the colour.

Rigid surfaces including medium-density fibreboard, hardboard, plywood, paper-coated cardboards, glass, plastics and metals will also require experimentation to check their absorbency. Be sure to check the quality of adhesion, which determines how well the wax sticks to the supporting surface. Wax paint may not adhere well to glass, and though MDF provides an excellent key it is extremely absorbent and will soak up lots of wax. Transparent support materials like clear PVC allow you to paint on one side and view the work from the other. Images created on clear materials can also be backlit to produce some dramatic effects.

Textured surfaces like rough watercolour paper, crinkled aluminium foil, natural wood, textured papers and boards offer interesting opportunities, but the wax may need to be applied in a different way. Experiment with different surfaces and techniques to produce some interesting effects.

Fabrics and **tissue papers** are highly-absorbent and extremely flexible. Images can be transferred to these materials by creating artwork on sealed lightweight card, then printing with them. Fabric printed like this can be embroidered by hand or machine, over-painted or made into a collage. It is suitable for decorative applications like wall hangings, but not contact items like clothing or furnishing. Silk and fine cotton produce the best prints because the weave is so close, but you should experiment with other materials to explore the many possibilities.

Above: the range of different surfaces which can be used for encaustic art work is limited only by your imagination. These include papers in different weights in absorbent and non-absorbent qualities, including different colours of paper and card; tissue paper; parchment paper; textured board; canvas and MDF (medium-density fibreboard).

USING COLOUR

The techniques for colour mixing with molten wax are similar to those used for any other art medium. Primary school basics apply: red and yellow make orange; red and blue make purple; blue and yellow make green. Different pigments influence the viscosity of colours: as a rough guide, lighter colours are runnier than the darker ones. The secret is understanding which red, yellow, or blue will give the results you want.

The lighter colours are usually runnier than the darker ones.

 27 *clear wax medium*

 16 *white*

 15 *black*

 14 *yellow brown*

 12 *red violet*

 09 *blue*

 10 *ultramarine*

 08 *blue green*

 23 *olive green*

 05 *lemon yellow*

 04 *golden yellow*

 02 *vermilion*

 01 *crimson*

MIXING COLOURS

Many different hues and qualities can be mixed. A 'true' red, mixed with a 'true' yellow, will give a clean orange. If the red contains any trace of blue, however, the orange produced will be browner and more muddy; if the red tends towards yellow the resulting mix will be lighter and brighter. Add white to create pastel shades and black for darker tones.

Above: the colours used to produce the wheel are crimson, lemon yellow and blue.

COOL TONES

 31 pastel blue

 19 cobalt blue

 10 ultramarine blue

 9 blue

 18 Prussian blue

 23 olive green

 8 blue green

 32 pastel blue

 11 blue violet

 6 leaf green

 7 green

WARM

These are the 32 Encaustic Art wax block colours used for the projects in this book. They are light-fast and totally intermixable.

 24 pink

 12 red velvet

 2 vermilion

 1 crimson

 5 lemon yellow

 4 golden yellow

 30 pastel orange

 3 orange

 13 rust brown

 25 gold metallic

 28 bronze metallic

 20 yellow ochre

 14 yellow brown

 21 Venetian red

NEUTRALS

 29 pearl medium

 26 Silver metallic

 22 umbra brown

 27 clear medium

 16 white

 17 grey

 15 black

COOL

Bluish and greenish tones are considered cool, and tend to 'recede' the painted areas they occupy. Hues can be made cooler by adding blue, green or white to the mix.

WARM

Reddish and yellowish colours are considered warm and tend to 'come forward' in a painting. Hues can be made warmer by the addition of some red, orange or yellow to the mix.

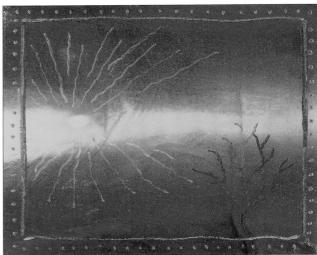

TRANSLUCENT

Some wax colours are *translucent* (light passes through them). Adding extra clear wax increases a colour's translucency. These colours offer great scope for painting and glazing in thin layers. They are affected by what is beneath them, and appear brightest over a white surface.

OPAQUE

When light bounces directly off the surface without any significant penetration, a colour is opaque. Wax opaque colours can be used for over-painting, in which the colour beneath is hidden by the new application. Layers can also be scraped through to show colour beneath.

MONOCHROME

Images made up of tones of just one colour are *monochromatic*. The results can emphasise style and contrast, like a black and white or sepia photograph.
Note: monochromatic images can be made up of tones of any single colour, not just black and white.

TONAL VALUE

One way to assess *tonal value* – the degree of darkness or lightness of an area – is to look at your work and begin to close your eyes: the more you close them, the more noticeable the contrast between light and dark.
Note: shades of different colours may have the same tonal value.

BASIC TECHNIQUES

A wax-coated surface is the basis for encaustic art painting: it is well worth carrying out a few 'practice runs' to make sure you can coat the surface of your card or other material evenly.

    When you are loading your iron, remember that the various shades of wax have different viscosities, i.e. some are thick and some are runnier. As a general guide, the lighter colours are more liquid than the darker ones – see page 16.

You will need
Lightweight sealed card
Iron
Waxes in three colours
Soft tissue pad for buffing
Clean disposable paper

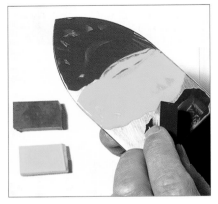

1. Protect your work surface with paper. Switch on the iron at a low setting and heat for two minutes. Load the base plate generously with three different colours.

2. Place the iron on the card and wiggle it slightly to make sure you have contact with the surface. Spread the wax evenly across the card to produce three stripes.

3. Place the iron flat on to the wax, then lift it off immediately, raising one edge first as though you were opening the lid of a box.

4. Holding the edge of the iron at a 45-degree angle, cut through the wax by gliding forwards to produce lines and a star effect.

6. Clean the iron to prepare it for the next use by wiping it with a pad of folded soft tissue.

5. When you are happy with the effect you have produced, wait ten seconds for the wax to cool. Buff the image to a sheen using a pad made from folded soft tissue paper.

Safety warning

Careless handling of the iron or dribbled molten wax can cause mild skin burns. If this should happen, hold the affected area under cold water for five minutes. Lavender oil is a great healer for burns.

Note: if pain persists, consult your doctor.

The completed exercise
Smoothing, lifting, edge and point markings form the basic 'alphabet' with which to start your exploration of these wax and iron techniques.

CREATING PATTERNS

Patterns are simply repeated or ordered marks. Dabbing, shuffling, wriggling and rattling may sound like the chorus of a pop song, but if you practise them, you will soon be able to devise and master new ones.

DABBING

Load the iron with two colours of wax. Dab over the whole surface using a lifting movement. Reload colours when necessary. When you are happy with the image you have created, allow it to cool for at least ten seconds, then polish very lightly to a sheen with a pad of folded soft tissue.

SHUFFLING

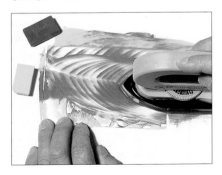

Load the iron with wax as in the previous step. Work from one side of your image to the other, shuffling the iron backwards and forwards in small steps as you go, to produce the effect shown. Let your work cool, then polish it as in the previous step.

WRIGGLING

Load the iron with two colours of wax. Move the iron backwards and wriggle the tip sideways at the same time, creating a zig-zag trail. Repeat until you are happy with the set of marks made, then let your work cool and polish to a sheen as before.

RATTLING

This great effect is formed by the edge of the iron, not its flat base plate. This method involves rocking the iron on alternate edges, using the pointed end as the pivot and keeping the straight rear edge of the base about an inch (2.5cm) above the work surface. While you are rocking the iron in this way, move it slowly backwards and away from the newly-formed patterns, without losing contact with the surface of your work. If this technique turns out to be more difficult than you expected, you can always refer to it as battling!

1. Load the iron with three colours of wax. Swipe from left to right to produce broad stripes of colour across the card.

2. Work over the whole card, moving the iron up and down so that the colours begin to merge.

3. Hold the iron loosely and rock it from side to side, using the point as a pivot as you move the iron backwards.

4. Repeat across the surface of your picture. Let the wax cool, then buff the surface to a sheen.

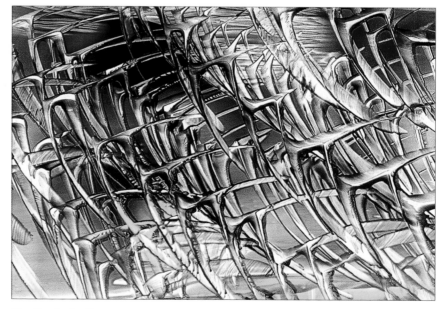

The finished effect

COMPOSITION

The word composition means *assembly* or *construction*. Many everyday tasks offer the chance to practise the creation of pleasing balance: arranging flowers, laying the table, landscaping your garden, planning the layout of a room or organising your desk. You can develop your skills by looking at good photographs or paintings – but remember that there is no absolute right or wrong.

Often, a composition is created by dividing the picture into thirds and placing major features on these imaginary lines. Sometimes shapes like a triangle, circle or an open 'L' can be used successfully to group the elements of a composition. The more you look around and experiment with images and photographs, objects and space, the easier it will become to identify good or poor composition.

A good exercise is to work on an inexpensive pad of drawing paper with a marker pen. Draw or scribble in a simple design of lines, shapes or areas. Work quickly, seeking a sense of balance in the final result. Make lots of drawings, keeping the ones which feel right and altering those which seem to have failed, in an attempt to develop and improve them. Practice will improve your eye.

Abstract on watercolour paper
The waxes were 'drummed in', or worked into the surface with the iron until they were absorbed completely, to create a harmonic background with a slightly lighter centre area or focal point. The scribbles with the stylus are roughly on the 'thirds' lines, and the low horizontal line (roughly a third up from the bottom of the picture) keeps the composition grounded. The taller, left-hand scribble is balanced by the shorter, but fatter scribble. The white dot gives more weight to the right side, and extends the horizontal line.

Lightning tree

Guidelines for good composition are evident in this landscape.
It may seem that I have deliberately overplayed the technique, but
I have been thinking about composition for so long that it has
become almost automatic. The field begins roughly a third of the
way up the picture, and the brilliant area of sky begins roughly
a third of the way down. The tree is roughly a third in from the
left, and the fence ends a third in from the right. The strong sky
was rubbed through while the wax was still warm to create the
burst of light. The tree — and the fence which encourages the eye
into the bright area — were added with the stylus.

MONOCHROMATIC BALANCE

The eye is naturally attracted to the area of strongest light or the most vibrant colour. This tendency for the eye to be drawn to an area provides opportunities for manipulating a response to a composition. 'Star-bursts' of light, as seen in the image opposite, help to keep the eye directed to a particular area. A word of warning: if you create this area of strongest attraction too close to an edge, it can lead the eye out of the composition. If, however, the area of powerful light or strong colour is kept within the central 'third' section, the focus remains firmly within the composition as a whole.

Different colours, for example blue and brown, may have very similar tonal values. If you look at the images below and opposite through half-closed eyes, until the fine detail becomes blurred, you should begin to understand the tonal values more clearly. In the picture below, the blue sky and the lighter brown areas of mountain have a very similar tonal value.

In the picture opposite, the stronger brown at the edge of the path has the same tonal value as the blues in the castle, mountain ridge and the sky area on the left. The soft brown at the edge of the star-burst of light is similar in tone to the pale blue towards the top right-hand corner. The tonal qualities of the composition have been balanced by adding the castle structures on the 'virtual line' a third of the way across the picture, to compensate for the dark, heavy section on the left. The foreground patterning in the lower left-hand corner was toned to balance the visual effect of the overall image. The weight should not be too far towards either side, or the image will seem lopsided, top-heavy, or just generally disquieting.

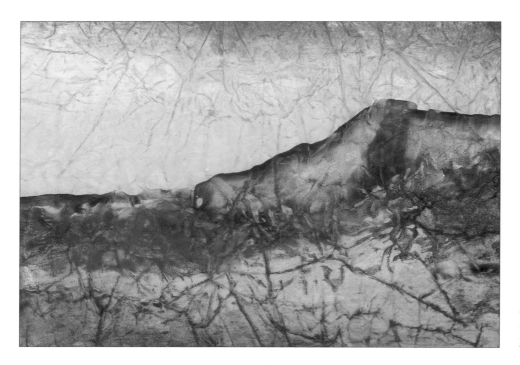

Landscape
A simple blend of colours on crushed paper has produced a dramatic effect.

Fantasy landscape

The focal point of this picture is just below the twin-peaked central mountain, because the eye is drawn to where the radial 'light beams' would converge. The tall peak and the castles frame this area and balance each other in stature and visual weight. The actual subjects of the picture — the mountains and castle — are irrelevant: it is the way in which the elements balance each other that makes it a satisfactory composition.

LANDSCAPES

Encaustic art is very forgiving, and allows you to 'rescue' virtually any card, even if you have made a complete mess of it. It is reassuring to know that, until you have sealed your work, you can change any piece of encaustic art at any future time.

Landscape is structured in three main bands: the light sky area; the distant horizon and the foreground. The shape of the horizon line that separates the land and sky determines the type of terrain: flat; low hills; high hills or peaks. Follow this exercise to turn an abstract practice piece into a convincing fantasy landscape.

You will need
Iron
Soft tissue pad
Waxes
Previously-worked card

1. Start with a card which has an all-over design. It can be one which has been overworked so that the effect is not pleasing.

2. Heat the iron and pass it smoothly across the surface of the card to re-melt the wax. Do this slowly, two or three times.

3. Working quickly while the wax is warm, wipe most of the colour off a band at least a third the width of the card for the sky.

4. The basic horizon is now ready for pushing and shaping into contours with the iron.

5. With the rounded edge of the iron, work over the lower portion of the card to push the wax up into the sky area and create a curved, hilly horizon.

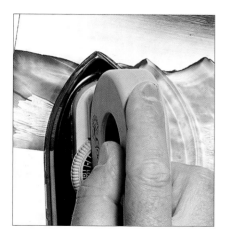

6. To create the impression of peaks, push the wax upwards with the point of the iron. Add more wax if necessary.

7. Hold the card against the base plate of the iron, making sure the top edge of the iron does not touch your work. Supporting the card with your fingers to control the point of contact, dab the surface of the card with the iron to add foreground texture, adding more wax if needed.

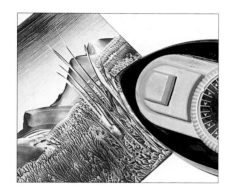

8. Add a grass effect by pressing and sliding forwards, cutting into the wax with the iron's edge to produce slightly curved lines.

9. Add a bird by picking up a spot of dark wax from a block with the iron point. Place on the sky and flick it quickly outwards, first one side, then the other.

The finished piece

ADDING DETAILS

The stylus tool maintains a steady, low tip temperature that is ideal for melting and applying wax colours. Depending on which tip you decide to use, it can offer the control of a pen (drawing tip), the blending ability of a brush (brush tip) and the facility to produce a variety of special effects (micro tip).

For even more variety, anything made of metal can be inserted in the stylus tip provided it is small enough and can be held firmly by the retaining screw. Experiment with screw heads, copper wire and other small metal items.

Any special drawing or representation requires some knowledge of the subject you wish to portray. While some flowers can be portrayed impressionistically, for more accuracy you will have to carry out a closer study. Use reference books or take photographs from nature; digital cameras are great tools too!

Picking up the wax

Let the stylus heat up for five minutes. Hold the tip on the wax block until it melts in and fills the slot with wax.

USING THE STYLUS

The drawing tip can be used like a pen. The slotted side must connect with the surface or the wax will not flow.

The brush tip can be used to 'paint' with the wax. Do not push into the wax block too hard, as it will ruin the tip.

The micro tip is shaped like a small iron, and can be used like the tip of a palette knife to move the wax around.

FANTASY FLOWERS

Imagination is a powerful tool, and the beauty of fantasy art is that no-one can say: "That's wrong". How would they know? Be creative and let your ideas blossom.

DAISIES

Are all daisies white with yellow heads? Do they grow in groups or alone? How big are their heads? When do they flower? Is a light or dark background better? Use a drawing tip for small work, or the brush tip for a single flower.

FOXGLOVES

Best-known for their slender magenta spires, foxgloves actually come in a multitude of hues. Finding out what plants live with them in the wild helps to create a realistic environment. All these were worked with the drawing tip.

COW PARSLEY

Tall plants can give your work form; a detail of a head in the foreground, one or two clumps in the middle distance, and a few spots suggesting far-distant flowers can add depth and interest. The drawing tip was used for this example.

POPPIES

What colour are poppies and where do they grow? How do they look in bud, when they first open, and in full bloom? The drawing tip was used for detail and the brush head or micro tip for larger flowers.

TREES

Many landscape scenes include plant growth, so trees can become an important element. The 'skeleton' of branches and trunk provides the basic shape. This example is of a basic structure showing how single branches split into two, and then into two again as you move upwards.

Be sure to explore some of the many other tree forms. A quick flick through any reference book on trees will show you how foliage varies at different times of the year, providing extra inspiration for your work.

You will need
Card
Stylus and drawing tip
Wax

1. With the stylus, draw in a simple balanced framework for the tree, dividing the branches at intervals to make smaller branches. Moving upwards one becomes two, and these in turn also divide.

2. Work over the tree shape, working backwards to thicken up the bases of the branches, noting that where two branches meet they become thicker.

3. Decide where you want the shadows and highlights to fall and add them to the sides of the branches with lighter and darker shades of wax.

The basic tree shape has been worked over with a dry stylus tip to blend the wax. Try to keep the composition balanced.

CREATING FOLIAGE

The leaf forms of different species vary immensely. Here are a few ideas on how to begin 'clothing' the basic tree forms. Study the foliage of different trees to decide which technique is the most appropriate. The handle of the iron can be removed so it can be used as a small hotplate or heated palette – see page 90.

STIPPLING

Load the metal brush tip by resting the tip in the wax. Lift off the colour and rough stipple in the basic tree shape. Move the wax round still stippling, to produce light and dark effects.

DOTTING

Convert the iron into a mini hotplate (see page 90). Melt and blend different shades of wax on to the upturned plate. Dip a natural hair paintbrush into the wax and dab on to the card.

PAINTING

Load the wire brush head with dark green wax and draw a line upwards from the bottom; clean the brush with tissue, then drag the line of wax into the branch forms using smooth, even strokes.

If an area looks too dark, clean the hot brush head and use it dry to re-melt and lift off colour.

You can often see through gaps in the foliage of a tree, so leave some blank spaces here and there.

To finish the fir tree, add 'skirts' which become larger and darker towards the bottom, giving the impression of weight and shadow.

SIMPLE LANDSCAPE

The simplest form of landscape could be represented by a picture with a light top section and a darker lower section. For a more interesting effect you need to blend colours for the sky and reflect them throughout the image: the sky does, after all, provide the light by which a scene is lit. The various shapes which can be created on the horizon line will dictate the 'flavour' of your landscape, for example flat, low hills, high hills or peaks.

You will need
Scrap paper
White card
Iron
Waxes
Soft tissue paper

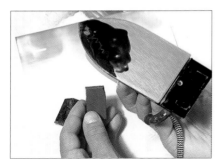

1. Load the iron with white, then pastel blue, then blue wax.

2. Smooth the iron across the top half of your picture. If it does not look right the first time, do not worry – just go over it again to blend the waxes until you are happy with the effect.

3. Clean the iron with a pad of soft tissue. Load it with olive green and yellow brown wax.

4. Place the loaded area of your iron on the card and smooth it across, cutting through the lower edge of the sky to add the horizon and upper contours of the hills.

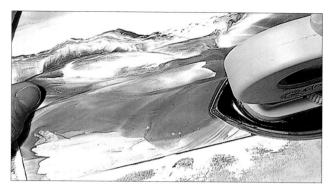

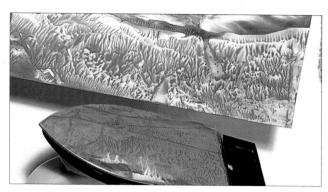

5. Continue smoothing the iron flat on the card to fill in the middle ground. If it begins to look dry and scratchy, add more wax to the base of the iron.

6. Add the foreground texture using the dabbing technique shown on page 22. Include a little of the darker sky colour to improve overall colour harmony.

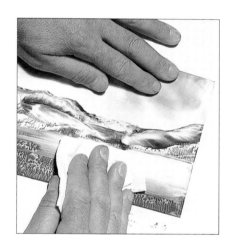

7. Working quickly before the wax sets and holding the card firmly, flat to the work surface, wipe away some of the wax to represent the water using one or two quick, sharp rubs, parallel to the card's lower edge.

8. Using the dabbing technique, tidy up the foliage at the water's edge. Add grasses using the edge of the iron and a cutting action, like the edge of an ice skate.

The finished landscape
The birds were added to the sky with the point of the iron, using green and brown wax together. Flowers were added, again with the point of the iron, in pastel blue with a small amount of darker blue for shading and colour harmony.

PLANNING YOUR LANDSCAPE

The sky colour and shape of the horizon line determine the mood and geography of the image. The iron can produce wonderful blends of colour in just a few simple strokes, yet also offers a surprising amount of control and accuracy.

Almost any imagined landscape form can be achieved, but remember it is far easier to respond creatively and intuitively to an image as it develops than to work to a plan, which relies on skill. If you try to plan a picture and it does not turn out as you hoped, you might consider it a failure. If you work creatively, developing the myriad forms that spring from your efforts, the images will prove interesting, adventurous and satisfying.

Often, the best approach is that of opportunist: just get started on the sky, see what sort of light it produces and choose a horizon shape which suits the feel of your picture. A flat horizon is calm, while a jagged effect can be almost a barrier to the eye.

Representational paintings are deceptions, in that what you acknowledge as realistic is actually based on illusion. There are many tricks you can learn to help the illusion succeed, but sometimes you can try too hard. The image above has been overworked slightly and has become too uniform, leading to a confused sense of focus.

Above: in this cool image, the main forms — mountain peaks, tall triangular foxgloves and spiky firs — are echoes of each other.

Opposite: the warm colours of the foliage and poppies give this picture a summery feel. The different elements, birds, trees and flowers, are repeated on a smaller scale to enhance the illusion of depth.

37

Passing clouds

Painted on glossy white card, this wide-open space is created using mainly white wax, with just enough stronger dark colour to give the distant mountains power and solidity. The low, narrow band of land is peaceful and calm, contrasting with the wild, windy action of the sky

Close to Spring

The sky was created before the horizon line and middle ground were added. The direction of the light in the picture then became evident, and the foreground was added. The tree reflects the direction and intensity of the light: it is dark in the shadow areas and quite pale on the illuminated faces. Several of the branches stretch out and point toward the light source. The stream reiterates this direction, creating a natural path for the eye to follow. The dots of colour that suggest flowers darken and increase in size towards the foreground, suggesting a sharper and more focused view of this area.

created for a series of greetings cards

39

ABSTRACT DESIGNS

Patterns and abstracts of assorted shapes and colours are fast, easy and fun to create. Blending harmonic colours produces particularly successful results. Cutting these abstracts up and rearranging them into more complex designs is both interesting and rewarding. When you have mastered simple squares, you can progress to more intricate arrangements including rectangles and triangles, rather like patchwork.

You will need
Stiff card
Finished artwork
Scissors
Spray mount or stick adhesive
Backing card

1. Select a range of finished abstract artworks in colours which complement one another.

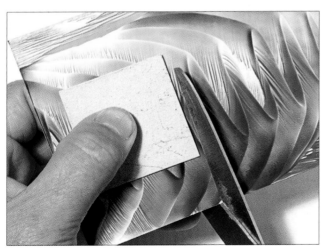

2. Make a square cardboard template and hold it over an area of a design which you like. Cut out a variety of squares in the same way.

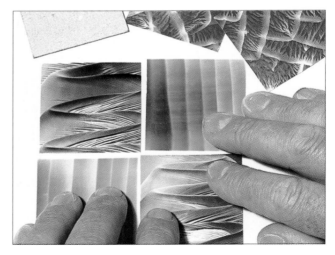

3. Arrange the squares until you have achieved a design which pleases you.

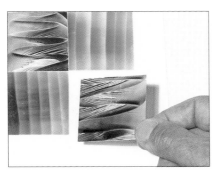

4. Stick the squares carefully on to a plain backing card.

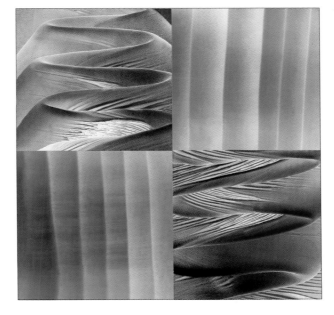

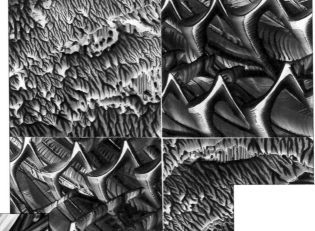

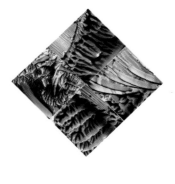

Abstract designs

A selection of completed designs. Mount a finished panel on plain white to make a simple but effective greetings card.

MARQUETRY CARDS

This approach to combining abstracts can lead to some surprisingly stylish results. The idea is to make a series of cuts through a fixed stack of two or more different abstracts, thus dividing each into identically-shaped pieces. Sections from different layers can be exchanged and reassembled to produce a 'jigsaw' of different-coloured designs. Keep it simple to start with, then when you feel more confident try more complex developments, using more cards and cutting each stack of cards into more pieces. When you are happy with an arrangement, stick it down on plain backing card with adhesive.

You will need
Cutting knife
Craft mat
Completed artworks
Plain backing card
Adhesive

1. Select two abstracts in complementary colours. Place cards one on top of the other on a cutting mat, overlapping them so you can cut through both layers at once.

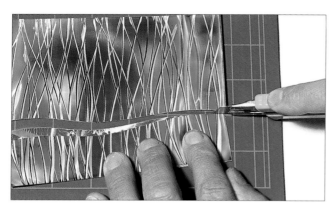

2. Score through both layers of card with a craft knife. Repeat the process to produce a thin strip down the middle of each card. These are now like two sets of identically-shaped jigsaw pieces.

3. Exchange the centre sections of the two sets of card pieces and arrange the strips into the finished designs. Note that this will produce two cards, each of which has taken its centre strip from the other.

Marquetry cards

Vary the amount of overlap to produce a wide range of different effects.

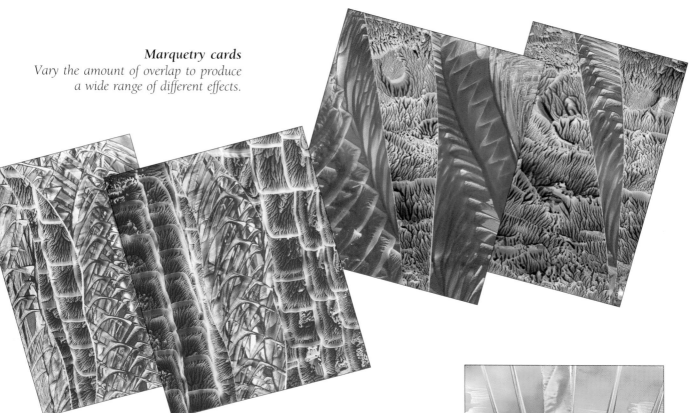

Choose dramatic contrasts to produce cards with completely different looks.

Fiery, hot colours clash with vivid yet cool blue, like refreshing water in a desert.

PATCHWORK MOSAIC

An assembly of variously-shaped and sized pieces can create something with far more impact than the original small cards. It is best to avoid complex designs when you begin to explore this idea: you may like to follow the example here and work on a square gridded outline. As your skill increases, so will the potential to build pictures using irregular shapes, combining the marquetry ideas shown in the previous project.

You will need
Stiff card
Pen or pencil
Semi-transparent paper
Selection of finished artwork
Low-tack adhesive
Rule or straight edge
Scissors
Permanent spray mount or adhesive

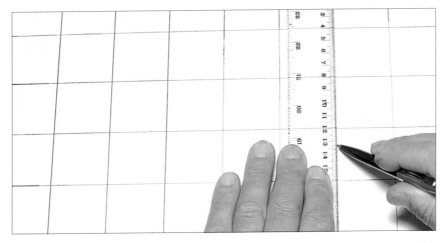

1. On stiff card, draw a grid to the size you want your finished artwork to be. Overlay a semi-transparent paper and draw out a design, making a variety of sizes and shapes from the guidelines underneath.

2. Cut out a range of shapes from finished artworks, varying sizes so they cover a different number of squares. Assemble them into a complete design, making sure the colours in your composition complement each other. Fix in place with permanent adhesive.

Tip
If you would rather plan your arrangement before fixing, use low-tack adhesive to hold the pieces in place temporarily. You will then be able to move them round without the risk of them flying everywhere.

STAINED GLASS

Strong coloured shapes defined by black lines are characteristic of stained glass, which when backlit looks vibrant and alive. Some encaustic wax colours are translucent. They produce colour vibrations which are very similar to those found in stained glass, and offer exciting design opportunities.

Almost any design can be treated in this way. Start your exploration with simple patterns like the example shown, or look at children's colouring books. Keep your eyes open for interesting images, and move on to produce stylised designs from ideas of your own.

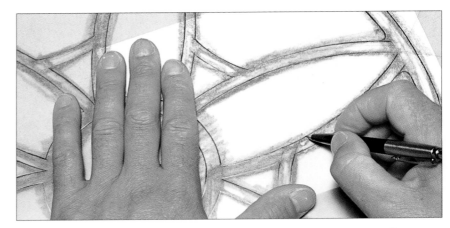

1. Draw out a design on rough paper. This one was drawn with the help of compasses.

2. Enlarge the pattern or blow it up using a photocopier. Transfer to tracing paper. Scribble on the back of the design, then use a firm point to trace out the shapes on to strong card.

3. Cut out your templates from the strong card. Place them on to finished artwork cards and cut out enough pieces to complete your design. Drawing out a rough layout will help to give you a feel for the composition of the piece.

4. Trace the design on to backing card. Stick down the pieces of artwork within the outlines. With the stylus and brush tip, lift off black from a wax block and paint in the outlines. These help to hide the joins between the pieces and add strength and definition to the final artwork.

Tip
Don't polish black wax too hard - it can smudge over the lighter colours and dirty them.

The finished artwork

SILHOUETTING

Another way to produce an attractive black edge effect is by drawing a silhouette on your card with a permanent marker pen. The marker pen stays in place when you iron the wax on to the card. Transparent waxes are ideal for this technique, as they produce a vibrant impression, almost like backlit stained glass, which contrasts well with the opaque black marker pen. Black absorbs all light, so translucent colours placed over it are virtually invisible. White reflects light and brightens translucent colour on white paper. Rubber stamps and computer clip art can provide good source material for silhouetting.

You will need
Permanent black marker pen
Transparent waxes
Clear wax
Iron
White reflective card

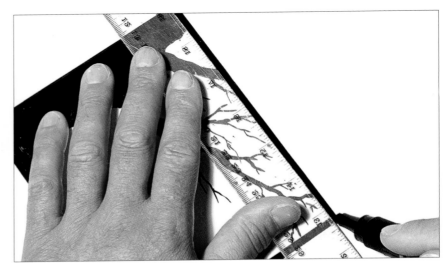

1. Plan out a design on card and draw it in using the marker pen.

2. Add a black line all round the edge of the design to frame it.

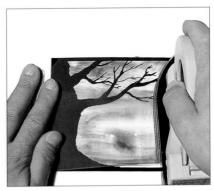

3. Cover the plate of the heated iron with unpigmented base medium (clear wax), which will thin the colours you add next and make them translucent.

4. Load the iron lightly with wax in pleasing colours – in this case purple, red, yellow and orange – adding them into the layer of translucent wax already loaded.

5. Spread the colours across the whole of the card. The silhouetted tree will remain black, and the white card will reflect the translucent wax colours.

Note

Black marker pen can also be applied *over* the wax of a completed card to frame it – see page 95 – or to create a silhouette effect, but a word of warning: if you try to re-work a card which has been finished in this way, the black ink will melt into the wax and you may be left with a mess!

The finished silhouette

PRESENTATION

Black borders like the ones on the examples shown can be applied to any encaustic wax artwork, either to the card before working, or over the top of the waxes. The crisp, strong border adds impact and definition, and can transform a finished piece from ordinary to remarkable.

Right: the cooler tones and simplicity of this portrait-format scene give it a tranquil feel.

Left: a combination of different techniques provide interest, and the green foreground complements and calms the warmth of the sunset colours, giving this artwork a Zen-like quality.

HOT AIR WORK

Any sufficiently-powerful heat source will melt the wax colours, so blown hot air offers many possibilities for moving the wax around. Try blowing ink across a card with a straw: if you blow wax across a smooth, clean surface it moves in a similar way. A different effect is produced if the surface of your support material is first covered with a layer of clear wax. Then, the colours applied and blown around on top will tend to 'flood' into surrounding areas. The technical details are complex, but it is very easy to experiment! All you have to do is take out your hairdryer and try it. Good luck!

You will need
Shiny black card
Stylus
Opaque waxes
Hairdryer

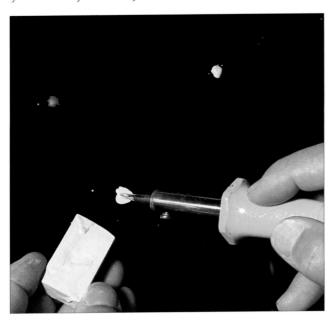

Note
When you first blow the wax in an attempt to produce this vortex effect, it may not go in the direction you expect. With practice the technique can be mastered and the results will become more controllable. The secret is to practise, practise, then practise some more.

1. Heat a stylus with a drawing tip and use it to take some wax directly from the block – see page 28 for the method. Drip the wax on the card to form a blob. Make several blobs in different colours on the card, leaving a space of a few centimetres between each. Clean the stylus every time you change colour.

2. With a hairdryer on the hottest setting, blow directly on to the wax blobs until they begin to melt and spread. Professional hairdryers are stronger and more controllable, and they do not cut out as their domestic counterparts tend to.

Fireworks

The blown wax spots are presented on black card, which makes them look like fireworks in the night sky. As a creative artist, you must first find an effect. Once you have discovered and perfected it, so that you can direct it with a degree of accuracy whenever you choose, you must decide how the forms should be interpreted and used. Below, the technique is used for a sky; on the following pages, it has been used for flower forms and a star-burst effect.

Sea and sky
The blown wax produces spectacular skies, but let it set first, then fill in the sea area afterwards.

Star-burst of light
This effect was achieved with blown wax on a plain white painting card. The lower section was tooled with the iron to create a stable landscape foundation for the castle. The tall, dark and sharp forms contrast strongly with the radiating light effect to make an immediate impact.

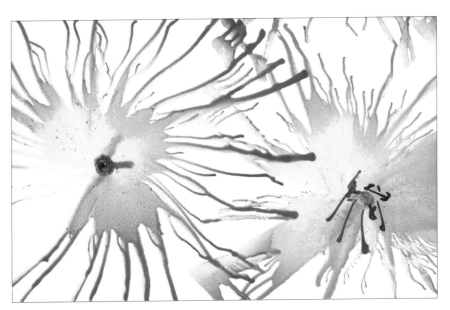

Flower forms
This spindly, blown effect was achieved by using a very powerful hairdryer to produce a strong blast of air to move the wax around as soon as it melts. The strange, straggly forms could also represent a type of sea urchin. For softer effects use a more gentle air flow, or pre-wax the card with clear wax which will encourage a more uniform coating.

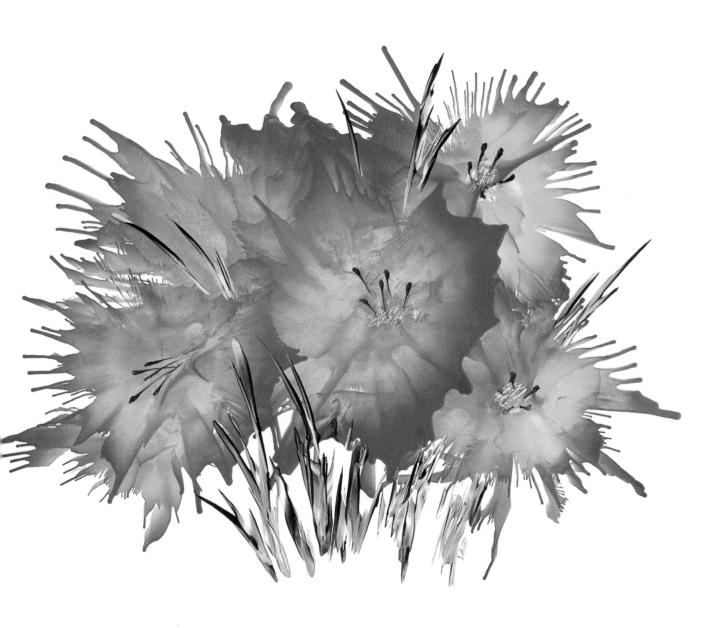

Flower forms

*To create these flower forms, several spots of wax were dripped on the
base card. Their centres show roughly where each blob was placed
before it was blown around. The wax spots were positioned close
together, so the blown areas have merged in places. The hot air thins
the wax as it blows out, so the colour looks lighter. Darker areas
show where the wax has been blown into a thicker layer, adding a
textural quality to the finished work. Hot air techniques can be
developed to create whole images and cover large background areas.
Ideal subjects include large sky areas, abstracts and fantasy work.*

DIFFERENT SURFACES

The easiest way to learn many of the basic encaustic art techniques is by using the iron and wax with non-absorbent painting cards. Re-working these cards is easy, so experimentation does not waste too much material. Remember, however, that the waxes can be applied to many surfaces, each of which interact differently with the waxes and reveal effects ranging from a muted hum to a loud, vital colour.

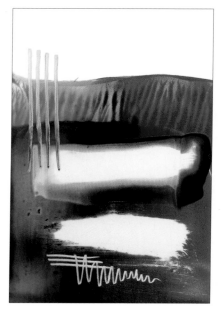

Non-absorbent surfaces like encaustic painting card do not allow penetration of the wax colours, so an area can be worked and reworked – at any time in the future – without showing any signs of previous applications. Remember that dirty wax colour can be re-melted and wiped off, as long as the sealed surface remains intact. With repeated working, the pigments may abrade the sealed surface, so eventually even sealed card will be soiled by marks which cannot be removed.

Partially-absorbent surfaces like copy paper, parchment paper or cartridge paper will allow some penetration of colour. Though some colour can be wiped off while the wax is molten, previous markings cannot be removed completely. The example above, which has been treated in exactly the same way as the first card, shows this clearly.

Some wonderful colour effects can be achieved: as a rule, if you apply lighter colours first, the final result will be cleaner and brighter.

Absorbent surfaces like cotton, silk or watercolour paper will quickly 'mop up' any wax colours applied. Interesting effects can be produced, but it will not be possible to remove the colour from the surface. See page 84 for details of printing on silk, page 86 for printing on cotton, and pages 72-75 for more information on using watercolour paper.

If work which has been done on an absorbent surface becomes too dark, light opaque waxes can be added to great effect.

Fantasy landscape
*Sealed card does not absorb the wax, so it allows you to create
incredibly vibrant pictures with glowing colours.*

Dawn fantasy

For this landscape on parchment paper, the sky area was completed before the horizon line and landscape details were added. The flash of light was removed in three strokes, with a pad of soft tissue wiped sharply across the sky area while the wax was still molten.

Landscape

The parchment paper used for the scene opposite gives it a softer feel than a hard, non-absorbent surface. Tints produced by the initial application of colour were toned down in some areas by wiping the molten wax with tissue.

SEMI-ABSORBENT PAPER

Open-surfaced materials will absorb colour. If the colour applied first *saturates* the paper i.e. fills the air pockets in its fibrous surface, it will stay in place when worked over with other colours. Splattered drops will therefore show through colours applied later, even if these colours are darker.

It is easier to obtain clean results if you pass the iron over each area of the paper's surface only once. On bigger work, you will need to stop and re-load the iron with more wax. Use more light colour than dark to begin with, or the artwork produced will be heavy right from the start.

Protect your work surface with scrap paper when flicking the wax and beware of over-enthusiasm – it should land on the paper, not the walls and carpet!

You will need
Wax colours
Semi-absorbent paper
Stylus
Drawing tip
Iron

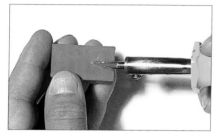

1. Heat the stylus. Place the tip on a wax block and hold in place until it melts into the wax, coating the tip of the stylus completely.

2. Flick the stylus quickly and quite sharply, so that drops of molten wax are scattered all across the paper.

3. Load the iron with several bands of wax colour. Hold it carefully at a right angle to the paper, so the wax dribbles down the baseplate. Press down across the paper – see page 60 step 3 – working carefully away from you, to melt the spattered spots of wax.

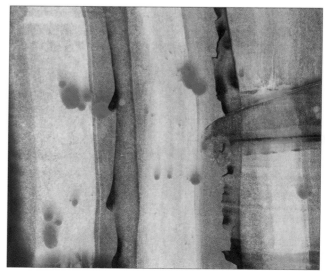

The finished picture, trimmed to shape.

JUDGING THE RESULTS

With this type of work, the piece as a whole may not be perfect. Sometimes just part of the work is really good, but if you lay blank paper over the parts you do not like, the good sections will quickly become apparent. Cut these out as smaller pieces of art, allowing a little extra border for easier handling.

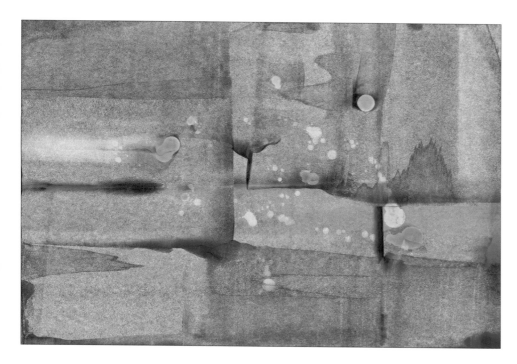

Abstracts

Results like these, on semi-absorbent cartridge or hot-pressed watercolour paper, are typical for early experiments with this technique. The absorbed colours have a softer feel, and the muted, even tones are easier on the eye than the harsh contrasts produced on sealed surfaces.

CRUSHED PAPER

Some interesting effects can be made by varying the texture of the surface you work on. An easy way to give your artwork a different look is to screw up a piece of paper, flatten it with your hand to smooth out, but not eradicate, the creases, then work on it. If you use paper which is coated to make it less absorbent, bruising or cracks in the paper's surface will absorb more wax and show as a network of fine lines.

You will need
Slightly absorbent paper (laser printing paper is ideal)
Wax colours
Iron

1. Crush a piece of paper by screwing it up in a ball. Open it out and flatten it with your hand.

2. Load the iron with your chosen wax colours, in this case blue, blue-green, red-violet and vermilion.

3. Place the straight edge of the iron on the paper at the nearest edge. Tilt the base plate so the waxes drip down in front.

4. Slowly, steadily and firmly push the iron forward, leaving a trail of absorbed colour. Repeat until the whole sheet is covered.

The finished effect. The molten wax has penetrated the areas where the paper was crushed. The dark veins which have emerged are reminiscent of a batik technique in which wax is applied to fabric, then cracked so dyes penetrate.

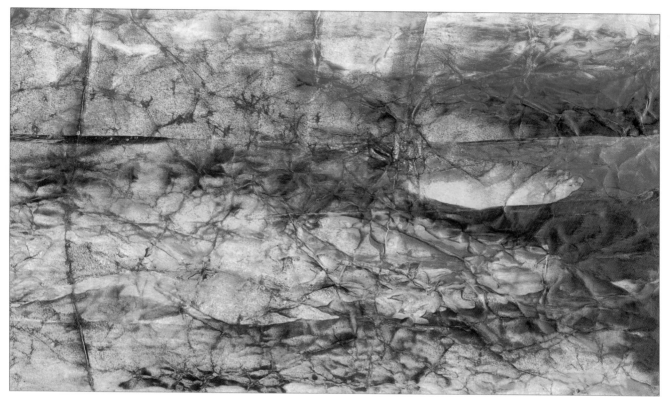

Crushed paper abstract

Wax on a screwed-up piece of paper – or lilies in a pool? Beauty is in the eye of the beholder, and while you are the creator, you are also the first to behold – and interpret – your creation.

Crushed paper abstract

Remember to include lighter colours in the initial or early applications. When areas have absorbed dark colours, applying light colours to them will have little or no effect.

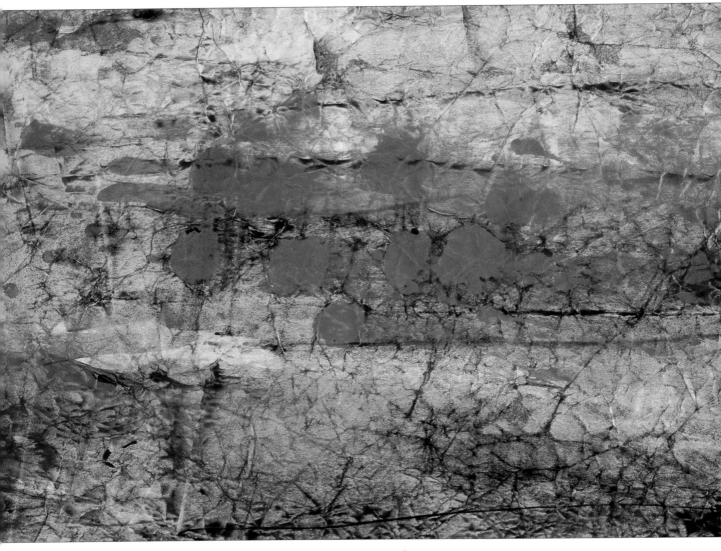

Poppy garden

This example shows how effective crushed paper can look after trimming to shape. The dribbling technique shown in the project on pages 80-81 has been combined with the crushed paper technique to produce this glowing representation of a garden in summer. Larger pieces of work will involve reloading the iron many times and working as cleanly as possible.

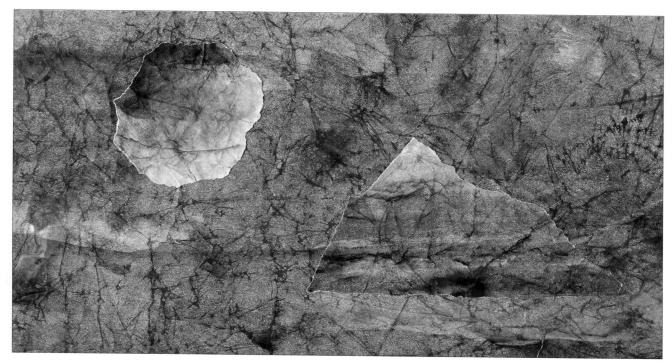

Snow-capped peak in a waxing moon

CRUSHED PAPER COLLAGE

Now that you have been brave enough to damage your paper before you even begin creating, why not take the process even further? Be really brutal and tear the finished work up as well! The results, even on simple collages like these, can be striking. Glue the torn pieces in place.

Desert temple

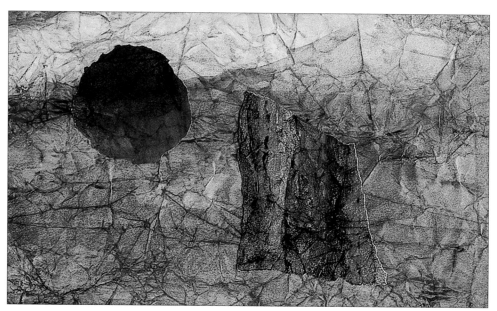

TEXTURED BOARD

Every type of surface has unique characteristics, though some make certain techniques easier to carry out, others may hinder them. Textured boards consist of facing paper bonded to support material which can range from thick card to hardboard. This rigid surface means that waxes can be built up quite thickly, yet remain stable. Many interesting surface patterns are available, with facing material ranging from non-absorbent to extremely porous. Techniques which can be used include iron, stylus, hot air, hotplate and applying molten wax with a paintbrush.

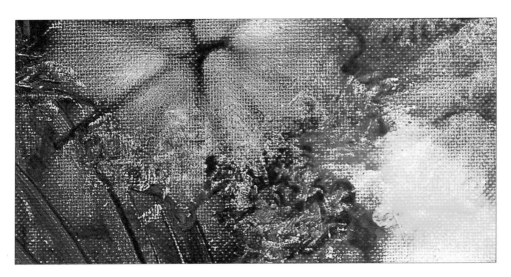

Detail
The enlarged detail, left, shows how the textured surface pattern shows through a thin layer of wax colour, however it has been applied. These markings can enhance your artwork by adding a subtle rhythm below the surface.

KEY POINTS WHEN CHOOSING MATERIALS

Absorbency: the capacity of the material chosen to absorb the coloured wax determines the potential to alter previous applications.

Surface colour: the colour of the support material or an underlying wax colour influences the reflective qualities and appearance of applied translucent colour.

Key: the amount of grip the surface offers to the applied wax

Flexibility: the potential of the support material to be crushed or bent, which will affect the number of application techniques possible.

Wax base: the type and proportion of ingredients used in a wax base influence its adhesion, malleability, clarity and durability.

Pigment type: light bounces off the surface of opaque pigment, while if you use translucent pigment, light enters the colour particles and creates a glow.

COLOURED CARD

White surfaces reflect light, while black surfaces absorb it. Different colours reflect their own part of the spectrum, and will influence the appearance of translucent wax colour applied on top. This means that a translucent wax colour will perform differently according to the surface to which it is applied. The card's surface colour becomes, in effect, the colour of the light within the piece of artwork. When translucent pigment colours are used, reflected light alters perception of the hue of the wax. Opaque colours are not affected because light bounces straight back off their surfaces.

Test card
Many colours of gloss card are available for experimenting with colour harmonies, contrasts and opposites. This example demonstrates how colour qualities and hues interact with a surface that does not reflect all colours equally. On this red card, green wax appears almost black (green is opposite red in the spectrum). Translucent yellow would appear orange, and red would hardly be visible.

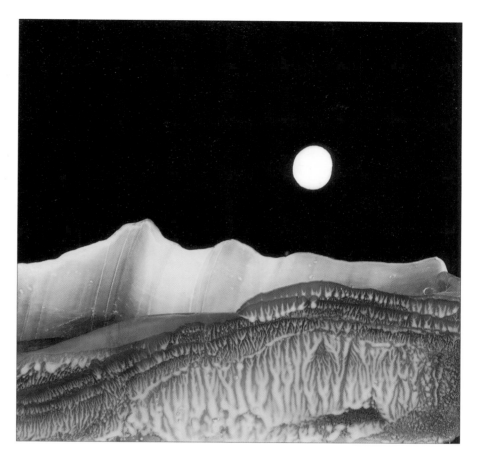

Moon over mountains
Black surfaces work well with opaque waxes of any colour. To create a nice round moon, let a single drop of molten wax fall straight on the card.

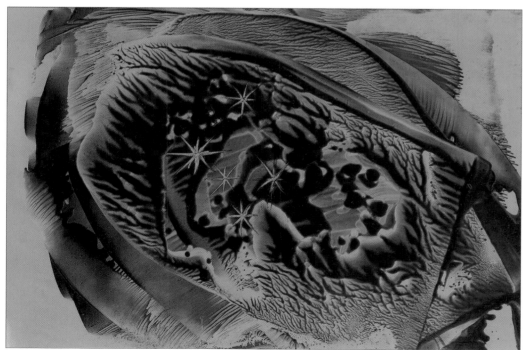

Incised abstract
Cards with metallic surfaces can be used as very effective 'scraper-boards'. First, coat the card with dark, opaque wax colour. Using a scriber tool, scrape and scratch off designs or drawings in the wax.

67

PEARLESCENT WAXES

Pearlescent and metallic waxes are well-suited for use on black or dark-coloured surfaces. The pearlescent wax may be tinted with any of the other wax colours to add interest and variety. The pearl effect comes from small plates of mica, a lustrous mineral which adds a subtle shimmering effect to the wax and is ideal for adding extra sparkle to fantasy backgrounds.

Silent flight
Simplicity often results in a strong and stylish outcome. The eye is not confused by too much information, and the mind can enjoy the spaces created, which leave room for emotion and for the imagination to flourish.

Ice palaces
The science fiction quality of the buildings in this example has been encouraged by using the stylus to add the unusual spirals to the towers. The trick is to make the image appear plausible, even if in reality such constructions may be impossible.

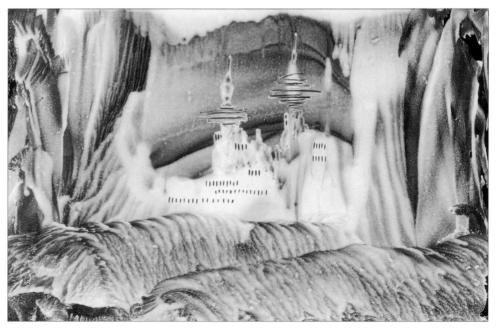

Crystal landscape

*Frost, ice and snow are an interesting subject, because with winter
landscapes an unusual reversal occurs. Instead of the sky giving
the light, it comes from the icy white earth, while dark and
gloomy hues fill the skies above. Here, iron effects dragged out of
the pearlescent wax on the surface of the black card are
embellished with the stylus, creating bare, icicle-covered branches.*

PARCHMENT PAPER

There is a pleasing softness in landscapes created on parchment paper. The surface offers qualities which are difficult to find in any other support medium. It is available in a range of soft colours, so you can explore various effects. It can also look extremely effective when backlit, i.e. with a light placed behind the artwork.

Parchment is virtually non-absorbent, yet it takes on a lovely, pale tint of the colours you have used. The general method of working is the same as with standard painting card. With care, it is possible to take a soft tissue pad and rub through the wax which has been spread on with the iron to reveal this pale tint. The rubbed area bears a faint memory of the colours that have been removed, and imparts a gentle glow to those that remain. Try it, and you will be surprised by the dramatic effects you can achieve.

Close up of effect

Scorched earth
Warmer colours, with no green, speak of barren places. Interesting forms were added; parchment paper allows changes if the initial effect is not pleasing.

Scottish landscape

Many people have thought that this landscape was painted in strong watercolours: the parchment gives that feeling to the wax colours. In this example, the sky was softened by rubbing with tissue; the hills were added with the iron and then were also softened a little in places using the same method. The area of water was smoothed on with the iron held flat, then the straight edge of the iron was gently tapped through the colour to create the impression of a ruffled surface.

WATERCOLOUR PAPER

All types of watercolour paper will absorb wax colour to some degree, but the smoother, hot-pressed qualities tend to take in less than the more porous types. Creative exploration and experimentation with different paper types should reveal some interesting approaches.

USING COLOUR

In this exercise, the yellow band of wax colour was applied to the watercolour paper first, and it has penetrated and saturated the porous surface. A second band of colours (green, blue and red) was then applied on top of the yellow, passing the iron from left to right.

You can see how the different colours behaved: the green has made little impression, but the blue and red have infiltrated and tainted the yellow with their own trails. In the bottom corner, the colours have been ground in ('drummed in') to produce soft, subtle shading.

Always test approaches and effects on a small experimental sheet of paper before embarking on larger pieces of work.

Opposite: Stylus work has been used to highlight this geometric abstract on watercolour paper.

Below: watercolour papers are available in a wide range of shades and different weights.

LANDSCAPE COLLAGE

This landscape collage uses torn strips of various qualities of watercolour paper treated by 'drumming in' the wax colours – see page 24. Choose colours appropriate to the areas of landscape you wish to represent e.g. green for grass or hills, soft blue for distant hills, blue and white for the sky. Dilute dark colours with clear wax before you spread them on the paper to avoid excessive tonal differences.

An assembly of torn pieces can be further enhanced by adding details with the stylus, 'crayoning' directly on to the design using the wax colours or over-painting with watercolours. Abstracts can work equally well, and you can experiment by criss-crossing the torn strips or cutting holes to reveal the layers beneath.

You will need
Various watercolour or absorbent papers
Wax colours
Painting iron
Permanent adhesive
Backing board

1. Load the iron with wax colours and spread over absorbent paper, grinding it in as you go.

2. Tear slowly and carefully across the paper to produce the shaped strips.

3. Build up your composition, adjusting the shapes and colours until you are satisfied with the effect.

The finished collage
The softness and control of colour that can be achieved using the 'drumming-in' technique offers many subtle and interesting possibilities. Combining different paper types brings a fresh and varied interest. The pieces have been fixed in place using permanent adhesive on a rigid backing board. The foreground has been enhanced by crushing the paper before applying the colour.

TISSUE PAPER

By 'tissue' in this case, I mean the boxes of two-ply soft paper you buy when you have a cold. It is a limp and fragile material, but if you first apply wax to rigid card or board, it can be ironed over and effectively 'glued' in place. Different textures can be created by ruffling the tissue during the ironing process, and another range of possibilities emerges.

TISSUE WITH METALLIC WAX

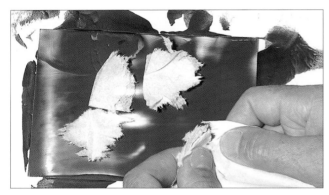

1. Melt and spread a good layer of darkish wax colour on a painting card. This is a good opportunity to use up old overworked cards. Tear up small pieces of tissue and scatter them over the wax surface.

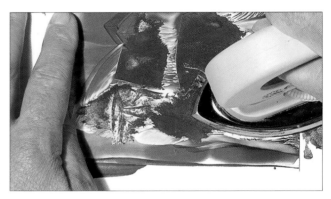

2. Iron over the tissue with care, so the wax underneath melts and saturates it. The tissue will become embedded in the wax and, when the wax is cool, it will be stuck to the base card.

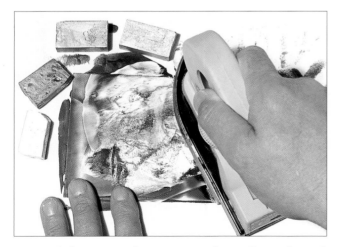

3. Load the iron with a mixture of metallic and pearl wax. Wipe it quickly over the tissue once or twice. The gold, silver, bronze and pearl pigments now sit on the surface.

4. Use scissors to cut out the most effective part of your design.

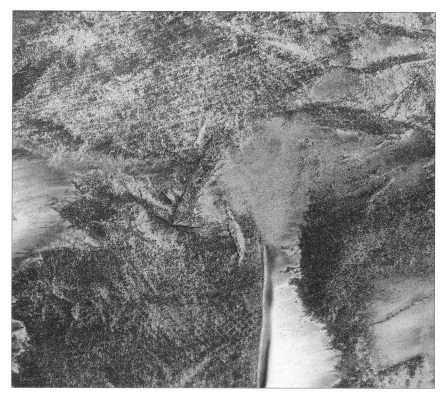

The completed square

Card with tissue squares

For the example right, several similar squares were mounted on a simple background. It would make an attractive greetings card, and one square could be used for a gift tag.

Left: Crayoned effect
Metallic wax colours provide scope for beautiful effects, and can also be used to crayon over the finished design to highlight the image.

77

COVERING LARGER AREAS WITH TISSUE

To cover larger areas for the creation of bigger pieces of artwork, it is both easier and more satisfactory to use whole sheets of single-thickness tissue rather than the small torn pieces used in the previous project.

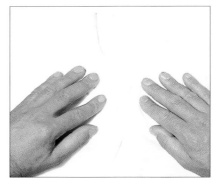

Creating a single tissue surface is very straightforward. Choose a piece of card or board the size you want your finished artwork to be. Use the iron to spread a good layer of clear wax over the entire surface, then separate your tissue into single layers and lay one piece of tissue on top of the waxed support. With care, because the separated tissue is very flimsy, iron over it until the underlying wax melts. Scrunch the tissue surface slightly with your fingertips before the wax cools and hardens. This should produce interesting textures of raised tissue ridges, which can be sculpted until the cooling of the wax prevents further change.

Sculpting the wax-soaked tissue

Work on top of the tissue-soaked surface, remembering that the colours will soak into the tissue and cannot be wiped off. Start with the lighter colours, such as the sky in the example below, then add the darker tones – the foreground in the example. The techniques may be simple, but the results can be stunning.

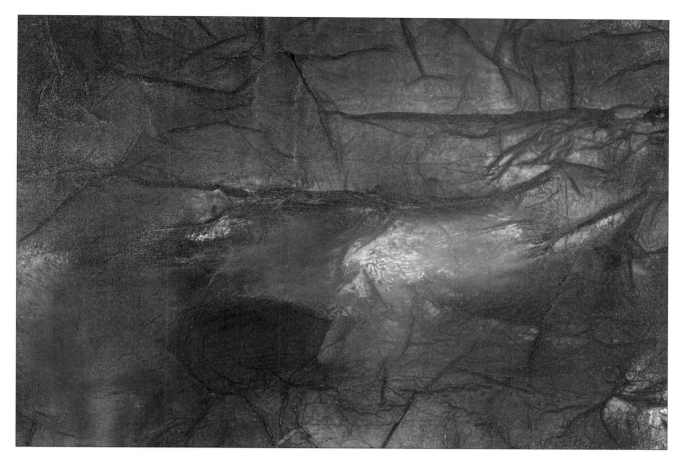

Tissue with metallic wax
Lighter colours are easily muddied if you overwork them. The example above could be enhanced with stylus work or used in mosaic, marquetry, patchwork or torn collage projects. It could also be printed on fabric and used as an interesting background for machine embroidery.

Crayoned sample
Raised, textured areas can be enhanced and highlighted by crayoning over them with the edge of the solid wax colours.

COMPOSITE BOARD

Using rigid substrates for encaustic wax work offers the freedom to apply thick 'impasto' effects, free from the risk of cracking and flaking associated with flexible surfaces. Suitable surfaces include thick card, hardboard, medium-density fibreboard and plywood.

A wide range of styles and surface effects can be achieved using layers of brushed-on wax in careful, light strokes or rough, heavy strokes. Applying molten colours using poured-on or dribbled methods can also yield some interesting textural forms and intensely-coloured areas.

You will need
Hotplate (upturned iron)
Paintbrush (hog's hair is ideal; synthetics may melt)
Waxes

1. With the iron assembled as a hotplate, brush molten wax on to the composite board.

2. Clean and reassemble the iron and melt wax on the plate. Hold the iron's point over the card and let wax dribble on to the surface.

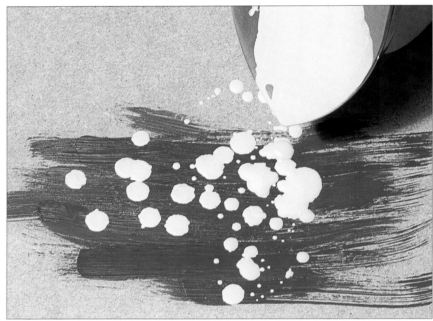

3. Put the iron back to hotplate format. Melt some green wax and brush it on to the surface.

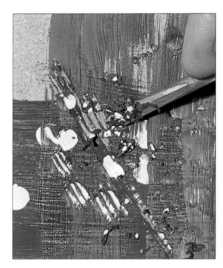

4. Use a scribing tool to scrape through the wax to incise a design and reveal the underlying layers.

Tip
To clean brushes, warm the fibres on the upturned iron, then wipe with tissue to remove most of the colour. Melt some clear wax on the iron, dab the bristles in and wipe again. This usually removes all the wax, but if necessary solvents can be used to complete the job.

The finished piece – an experiment in techniques

Note
To reduce the absorbency of composite boards, prime the surface with white PVA adhesive diluted with water. Use the proportion of 30 per cent PVA to 70 per cent water.

Artwork on composite board
The textures produced by brushing or dribbling the wax, or by carving or distressing the thick wax layers, bring a new dimension to encaustic art work. Large pieces are especially inviting, as the variations in surface texture provoke more than just the visual sense.

PRINTING AND OVER-PAINTING

Thick, absorbent watercolour paper will readily accept a print from a wax painting. This process alone can yield pleasing results and is a good way to capture detailed scenes on interesting textured paper surfaces. The wax on watercolour paper can be developed by over-painting with water-based colours like the example below.

You will need
Completed artwork
Iron
Tissues (Two-ply)
Watercolour paper
Watercolour paint
Palette
Brushes

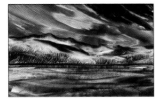

1. Select a completed artwork. Monochromatic pieces work well with watercolour, but make sure there is a good balance between the light areas (not much wax) and darker areas (heavier coating of wax).

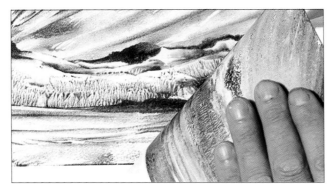

2. Lay the artwork face-down on watercolour paper. Lay tissues over the back of the card to protect the surrounding paper, then iron over it slowly to melt and transfer the wax. Peel off the original card while it is still warm or it may stick to the paper.

My watercolour palette

3. Over-paint the design with watercolour paint. The wax acts as a resist, so only the areas which have remained white will take up the paint.

The finished artwork

Colouring this landscape with washed-in watercolour results in a pleasing and interesting effect. There are many ways to use this water-resisting property, and many of the ideas previously covered can be adapted to suit: multiple prints, abstracts and torn and collaged pieces are just a few. In creativity there is no right and wrong: if it produces a pleasing result, it works.

SILK OVER-PAINTING

Silk is a beautiful, finely-woven material which takes a wax print very effectively, giving a crisp, clean reflection of the original. The interesting forms and effects of the wax print, combined with the shimmering vitality of silk paints, can produce a lively and intriguing artwork. Whether you choose to produce a simple print like the example shown, or a large area covered with a collection of printed impressions, creative boundaries are extended by this alluring approach.

Wax-rich areas of the printed image resist the silk colours. Try to avoid heavy or dark wax prints and take care to leave some light or white areas where the over-painted silk colours can shine through.

You need a stretching frame for this project, but you can make your own by up-turning a cardboard box and cutting out a rectangle from the base.

1. Complete an artwork on card, using a variety of techniques. Make sure that the print you choose is well-defined.

You will need
Small piece of silk
Soft white two-ply tissues
Iron
Cardboard box
Silk paint
Paintbrushes
Jar for water
Pins
Palette for silk paints (optional)

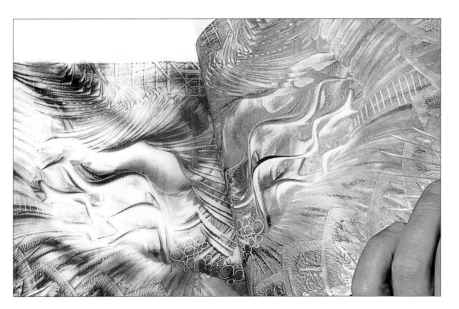

2. Lay the silk fabric on a bed of soft two-ply tissues, which will soak up any excess wax. Place the artwork face down on the silk and lay the tissues over it to protect it from any dirt on the iron. Iron through the tissues, pressing firmly all over to melt the wax, then peel it off. If the wax does not print off easily, turn up the heat of the iron and work over the print more slowly.

3. Pin the fabric on your frame. Paint the stretched silk using a round brush and silk paints, diluted if necessary. Take care not to overload the brush.

The finished painting

Silk-painted artwork
The interesting forms from the reversed wax original are visible through the bright translucent hues painted over the silken piece.

FABRIC COLLAGE

Encaustic wax colour can be printed from the non-absorbent painting cards on to fabric, to be used as a background for creative hand or machine embroidery or collage. Printing from images produces an obvious result: a softer, mirror image of the original artwork. To do this, place a couple of layers of tissue on a clean work surface to mop up any excess wax, and spread your fabric over it. Position the artwork face down on the fabric, cover it with a fresh tissue and iron over it firmly and slowly. Lift a corner to check that the design has transferred, then peel off. Compiling fragments of different artworks into a design can yield some unusual and interesting results.

You will need
Wax image cards
Fine-weave cotton fabric
Cutting mat
Sharp knife
Rule
Iron

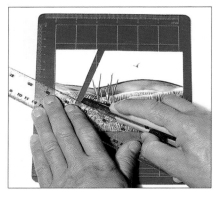

1. Decide on the general shape of the pieces you want to use and cut out sections from artwork using a knife and rule.

2. Spread tissue on your work surface and lay fabric over it. Lay a section of artwork face down and iron over it. Lift carefully to make sure the design has transferred.

3. Repeat the procedure to build up the design jigsaw-style. You may have to plan ahead to make sure pieces are the right shape to fit in particular areas.

Note
Encaustic wax work is for decorative effect rather than for clothing or furnishing, as washing will remove much of the colour. It is ideal for incorporating in wall hangings and other decorative pieces.

Fragments of a landscape
Fabric printing offers lots of creative potential, enabling the exploration of many different combinations of image. Further colour can be added using the wax blocks as crayons, or added with a stylus. Other options include over-painting with translucent washes of fabric colour or embellishing with embroidery.

EMBROIDERED DESIGN

On the previous pages, I discussed the use of wax to print images on a variety of absorbent surfaces. Fine-weave fabrics offer a detailed print, whereas rough, open fabrics only reflect loosely the colour areas of the original design. Whichever approach you choose, there is great potential for using these works as the background for creative embroidery. Use a machine for substantial thread additions, or sew by hand for a more subtle enhancement of your work. Textured or 3-D objects can be incorporated to increase the surface interest; beads, twigs and fleece are just a few of the possibilities.

embroidery in progress

Beaded abstract with gold thread
Embroidery is a great platform for creative experimentation. For extra interest, you can creat 3-D effects using tiny objects secured by thread, or even a hot glue gun.
embroidery by Jane Champion

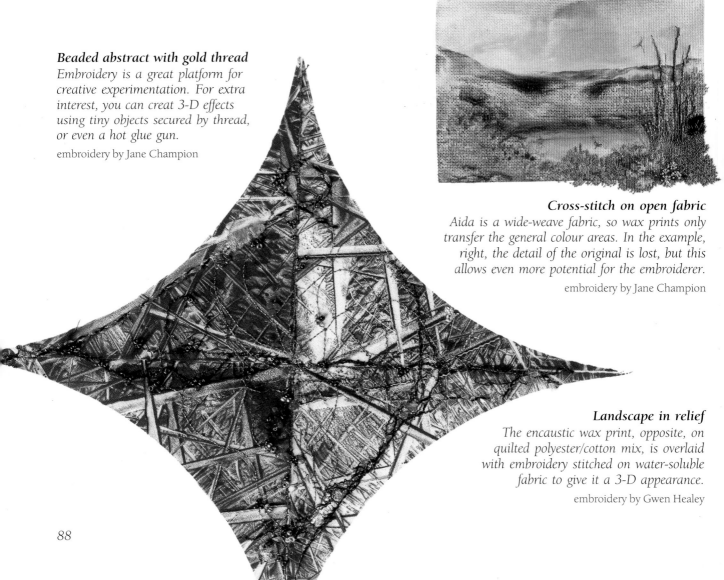

Cross-stitch on open fabric
Aida is a wide-weave fabric, so wax prints only transfer the general colour areas. In the example, right, the detail of the original is lost, but this allows even more potential for the embroiderer.
embroidery by Jane Champion

Landscape in relief
The encaustic wax print, opposite, on quilted polyester/cotton mix, is overlaid with embroidery stitched on water-soluble fabric to give it a 3-D appearance.
embroidery by Gwen Healey

WAX STAMPING

This technique inverts the usual method of applying wax to the card with a hot iron because it uses the iron as a hotplate. Turning the iron upside-down makes it into a mini-hotplate which provides a flat, level working surface. The card is placed on the iron and is worked directly into a final image.

Rubber stamps are particularly effective when used in this way. The molten wax allows fast duplication of images such as the tree below.

REMOVING THE WAX WITH A STAMP

1. Assemble the iron into hotplate form. For extra safety tape the base to the handle when the assembly is complete.

2. Hold the card flat on the hotplate. Wax it all over using yellow-brown in the centre and blue all round the outside edge.

3. Use the flat paintbrush to thin the wax in the central area of the card.

4. Press the dry stamp in the middle of the card. Hold it in place for a few seconds, then lift it off.

5. Decorate the edge by working around it, using part of the stamp and pressing it into the wax already on the card.

The finished artwork

Note
To clean the stamp, place it on the iron for a few seconds, then wipe it on soft tissue paper. Repeat until the stamp is clean.

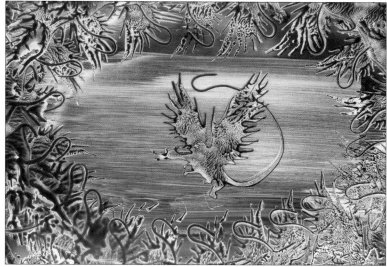

Cards worked using this technique are easy to rework until you are satisfied. The wax remains in liquid form while it is on the heat, so alteration, addition or removal is possible. Larger hotplates allow even more potential for the development of complex creative techniques.

WAX STAMPING - APPLICATION

Stamps can be coated with wax and printed on to a variety of surfaces. The stamp should be re-waxed every time it is printed off — see page 91 for an effective method of cleaning the stamp.

1. Place a card on the upturned iron to use as a palette. Add green and brown wax, in the rough shape of a tree, to the card and let it melt.

2. Place the stamp in the wax and hold it in place for a few seconds, moving it slightly to coat it thoroughly. Put the palette card aside.

3. Place a fresh card over the mini-hotplate and position the waxed stamp carefully. Hold it firmly in place for a few seconds, then lift off.

4. Use the excess wax from the edge of the stamp to create the foreground detail.

The finished tree

BORDERS AND FRAMES

Good presentation of your work can lift something ordinary into a higher art form, giving it more impact and making it more harmonious and interesting. Creating your own decorative borders gives you far more control over the impression an image makes, and even narrow borders can be extremely effective. Consider colour harmony and visual noise, making sure that the frame does not attract so much attention that it actually detracts from the artwork it is meant to complement? It is important that the border relates to the subject it frames, and do not forget that both aperture and frame can be any shape or size.

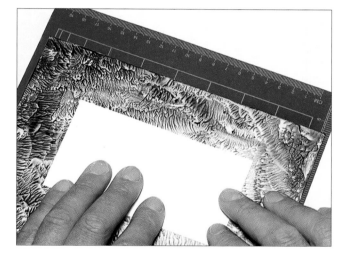

1. Use a scalpel and a cutting mat to cut out a piece of card slightly smaller than the artwork you want to frame. This is the template for the aperture in your border.

2. Choose a piece of finished artwork slightly larger than the one you want to frame. Place the aperture template in the centre of the artwork.

3. Cut out the aperture by running a scalpel round the edge of the aperture template.

4. Place your artwork under the frame and fix in position using adhesive tape.

Note
Although this example and those on the following pages have rectangular cut-outs, you can make the aperture any size or shape you choose.

Poppies
This abstract depiction of poppies in a landscape, left, is framed using a complementary artwork which was blown with a hairdryer. Mounting it off-centre creates extra interest.

Cityscape
The radiating lines round the frame add a sense of perspective to the view of skyscrapers. They were created by sliding the straight edge of the iron in carefully-controlled and angled strokes.

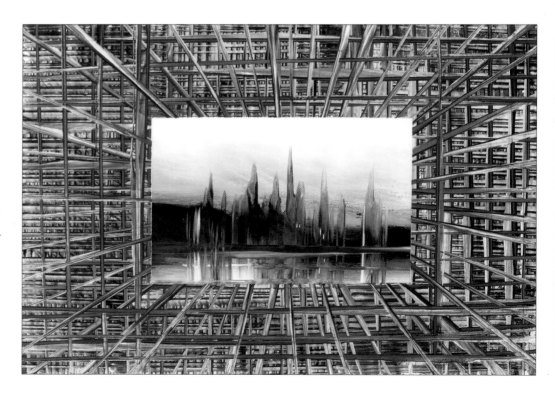

BLACK LINE BORDERS

All artwork benefits from good presentation: take a look round any art gallery and you will see carefully-mounted and framed works. Notice also the amount of space around each individual artwork. Space lets the eye rest and focus on a single image without disturbance from other visual sources, allowing the viewer to connect fully with the work.

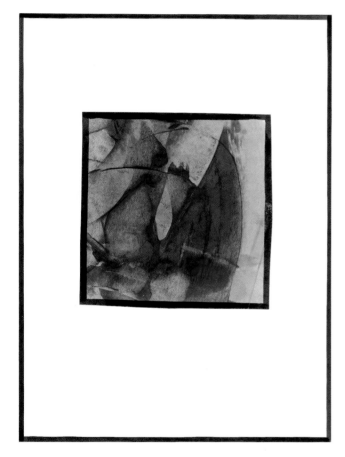

    A fast and inexpensive way to sharpen up the appearance of any finished piece is to add a crisp black line as a border. Do this using a rule and a black marker pen. You can work round the edge of a trimmed piece of artwork, or, if you use a permanent marker pen, you can apply the line directly on top of the wax. A word of warning: do not try to re-work a card marked with an ink border — the ink will blend with the wax and you may be left with a mess. Enjoy your encaustic art creations!

INDEX

Absorbent paper *see surfaces*
Abstracts   4, 5, 6, 7, 24, 28, 36, 40-41,
   61, 67, 72, 83, 94
Adhesive   10, 40, 42, 44, 46, 74, 81, 93

Board *see surfaces*
Borders   5, 49, 93, 95
Brushing *see techniques*

Card *see surfaces*
Cardboard *see surfaces*
Collage   5, 15, 63, 74, 83, 86
Colours
   contrast   19
   mixing   16
Composition   24, 25
Crushed paper *see surfaces*

Dabbing *see techniques*
Dotting *see techniques*
Dribbling *see techniques*
Dripping *see techniques*
Drumming in *see techniques*
Dyes   13, 60

Embroidery   79, 86, 88

Fabric *see surfaces*
Flicking *see techniques*
Flowers   6, 30, 31, 35, 37, 38, 51, 53
Focal point   24, 27
Foreground   26, 28, 29, 31, 35, 38, 49,
   74, 78, 92
Frames   5, 48, 49, 84, 85, 93, 94

Glue *see adhesive*
Grasses   35

Hot air   5, 50, 53, 64
Hotplate   10, 33, 64, 80, 90, 91, 92

Iron   4, 6, 7, 8, 10, 14, 20-23, 28-29, 30-
   31, 33, 34-35, 36, 48, 52, 54, 58, 60, 64,
   69-72, 74, 76, 78, 80-82, 84, 86, 90-92

Landscape   5, 25, 28, 32, 34, 35, 36, 52,
   55-56, 69, 70, 71, 74, 83, 86, 94
Light-fastness   12, 13

Marquetry   5, 42, 44, 79
Melting point, of wax   12
Monochromatic balance   8, 26
Monochromatic images   19, 82
Mosaic   5, 44, 79

Over-painting   4, 5, 15, 19, 74, 82, 84, 86
Overworked pieces   28, 36, 76, 79

Painting *see techniques for various papers*
Paper *see surfaces*
Parchment *see surfaces*
Patchwork   44-45
Pen, marker   13, 48, 49, 95
Pigment   12, 13

Rattling *see techniques*

Scribing tool   10, 80
Shuffling *see techniques*
Silhouetting   5, 48, 49
Silk paint   84-85
Sky   25, 26, 28, 29, 34, 35, 36, 38, 51,
   53, 56, 69, 71, 74, 78, 94
Stained glass   5, 46-47
Stamping   5, 48, 90, 91, 92
Stippling *see techniques*
Stylus   4, 7, 8, 10, 24, 25, 30, 32, 46, 47,
   50, 58, 64, 68, 69, 72, 74, 79, 86
Stylus tips *see tips*
Surfaces
   absorbent paper   7, 14, 00
   board   5, 14, 15, 44, 64, 74, 76, 78,
      80, 81
   cardboard   15, 40, 84
   crushed paper   5, 26, 60, 61, 62, 63
   fabric   15, 84, 88, 89
   parchment paper   5, 9, 14, 54, 70, 71
   rigid   4, 14, 15, 41, 64, 74, 76, 80
   semi-absorbent   5, 58, 59
   tissue paper   15, 76-79
   watercolour paper   5, 14, 15, 24, 54,
      72, 74, 82

Techniques
   brushing   64, 80
   dabbing   22
   dotting   33
   dribbling   62, 80-81
   dripping   50-51, 67
   drumming in   24, 72, 74
   edge marking   22
   flicking   58
   lifting   22
   painting   33
   point marking   22
   rattling   23
   shuffling   22
   smoothing   22
   stippling   33
   wriggling   22
Textured surfaces   15
Tips
   drawing   4, 10, 24, 25, 30, 31, 32, 50
   brush   10, 30, 31, 33, 46, 47
   micro   10, 30, 31
   mini   10
Tonal value   19
Trees   5, 6, 25, 32, 33, 37, 38, 48, 90, 92

Viscosity   16

Waxes
   colour range   12, 17
   metallic   76-77, 79
   opaque   14, 19
   pearlescent   17, 68
   translucent   18
   types of   13
   viscosity   16, 20
Wax sealer   13
Wriggling *see techniques*